I AM Creating My Own Answers

by
Barry Thomas Bechta

UNCONDITIONAL
LOVE BOOKS

*Redefining, Guiding, and Inspiring Humanity's
Connection to the Creative Power within.*

I AM Creating My Own Answers
by
Barry Thomas Bechta

Library and Archives Canada Cataloguing in Publication

Bechta, Barry Thomas, 1968-
  I am creating my own answers / by Barry
Thomas Bechta.

ISBN 978-0-9686835-1-4

1. Self-realization--Religious aspects.
2. Spiritual life. I. Title.

BL624.B432 2009   204   C2009-905721-2

I AM
Creating My
Own Answers

This
book lovingly reminds
me to ask the question: What
would bring me the most Joy
and serve God in others
Right Here Right
Now?

ACKNOWLEDGEMENTS

I AM Eternally Grateful for God's Presence in my life. My Conscious Unification with each individualisation of God continually transforms my life in extraordinary ways. My world is Now GOD, Greatness Oneness Demonstrated.

I AM grateful to Binah C Godisall for the mirror she has become in my life. I wish for her exactly what she wishes for herself as we experience the freedom of Unconditional Love together.

My child like gratitude bubbles forth to Anthony and Zachary. They both have reminded me that it is all just a fun game we are playing. Especially our group hugs.

Loving thanks to Stephen, Margaret, Gabrielle, and Samuel for all their support as we continue to share our experience.

Warm thanks to my family by blood and by love. My Loving family grows in feeling each day.

I AM extremely grateful to all the authors that continually inspire me to challenge and expand any limits in my view of God, Love, and Life.

Special Thanks to John Randolph Price, Jamie Sams, Joe Vitale, and Neale Donald Walsch whose works I have throughly studied because of their ability to remind me of my Oneness with all that is God.

Thank you, Prince. Meeting you at Paisley Park and discussing the spirituality imbued in your music, particularly *The Rainbow Children* was electrifying and a dream come true.

Once again thank you to everyone who has ever helped me in any way over the years.

I love all of you very much.

TO THE READER

I *read* books to discover tools I can use in my life to make it easier.

I *write* books to Create a record of the tools I use in my life to make it easier.

Whenever I discover that my thoughts, feelings, words, or actions are getting me down, I pick up one of my books, open it anywhere, and the information I read reminds me that God Gives Ongoing Direction in my life Always in All Ways.

I Love the word: God. For me it perfectly describes the Energy of Life. God/Life/Energy are interchangeable words that encapsulate my belief in and experience of something that is simultaneously a part of me and apart from me.

I wrote *I AM Creating My Own Answers* as my personal Oneness Bible. Whenever I have a question in life, I pick up this book or one of the accompanying cards (found on the last pages) and they all remind me that my most empowering Answers to any Challenge I may have, encourage my Oneness with God/Life/Energy: *We Are All One.*

Choosing Unity over separation in my experience is the path to my peace and my healing. Choosing Love over fear in my experience is the path of Unconditional Love. When everyone Chooses Unity over separation and Love over fear the result is God, Global Oneness Demonstrated. I believe that we, as a world experience, are moving towards a vision of God/Life/Energy that Promotes and Supports Individuality and Global Oneness Demonstrated.

Over the years, the one practice that has transformed my life the most has been writing down my Consciously Chosen thoughts, feelings, words, and actions that Uplift and Encourage God's Joy and Potential in my life experience. I write out my beliefs in my books and read them to form my Conscious Habits. Habits can be Created or Changed by continually choosing them for as little as 28 days. I Choose to Consciously Create my Habits

I encourage you to begin writing your own Belief Bibles to Consciously Choose Heavenly Habits. Consciously Choose thoughts and feelings that Uplift and Encourage Joy and Potential in your life. Consciously Choose Only Habits that Encourage your

Dreams and Connection with God/Life/Energy. Release all Habits the Deny your Dreams and Connection with God/Life/Energy.

May God Richly Bless you, your family, and your friends as God Gives Ongoing Direction in your life through the Perfect people, places, and things always in all ways.

In Loving Oneness
Barry Thomas Bechta

TABLE OF CONTENTS

Everything happens
in the Perfect way
and at the Perfect time.

Most of the things that are Perfect
and for my Oneness
have a total calm and Relaxed feeling
associated with them.

When I AM Relaxed
I continue to Create
Relaxed experiences.

I AM RELAXED

Everything happens in the right way and at the right time, no matter what appears to be. When I AM Relaxed I continue to Create Relaxing experiences.

When I wake up each morning, I connect with The Feeling of God and take a moment to invoke a Relaxed state. I envision my day working out exactly as I plan with The Feeling of God. God is the Cause to all my experiences. God is the base to my perception of my experiences. God expresses God Self through me in all of my experiences.

From this Relaxed state I move through my day. Even if I seem to be running late, I know that The Feeling of God is directing my entire experience. If I am late for work, I Relax and take responsibility and call to report my tardiness. If I miss a bus, I Relax because there are other buses. If my appointment gets delayed, I Relax and accept that everything happens in the right way and at the right time.

Most times when I am late, miss a bus, or have an appointment delayed, I meet someone I would never have met had I been on time, made my bus, or kept the scheduled appointment. Sometimes the person I meet is someone I have not seen in a long time, or someone I had been thinking about recently, or someone I meet for the very first time. These people are there for me to connect with for a myriad of reasons which God knows.

The Feeling of God works on such grand scales that chance meetings are never really chance. I open to these experiences Now and I Never Overlook Whatsoever the opportunities provided through The Feeling of God. These experiences bring me into contact with the Perfect people, places, and things to help me move forward in my experience.

My experiences with these Perfect people, places, and things many times are the answers to prayers I have given, or questions I have asked, or the guidance that can redirect my journey. These experiences may even come in the form of lessons that are challenging for me to receive, understand, and accept. The information may change me drastically from a position that I believe is secure to a position that is powerful.

No matter what experience comes to me I realize I can Choose and Create from it. To stay Relaxed I develop systems that allow me to be Centered in all my experiences. In situations that seem challenging I ask The Feeling of God to show me the opportunity. In experiences that I cannot understand I ask for guidance. As I use these systems in my life and trust in The Feeling of God to provide my answers I grow in my understanding of who and what I AM.

I develop systems for total Centered relaxation. I listen to my body and I AM aware of the areas where stress displays itself. If I feel stress in my arms or find that my hands are clenched, I take a moment to shake the stress out. If I feel words inside me asking to be expressed, I express them. When I feel a lull in energy I perform activities to energize myself. When I need to release sorrow, I cry. These seem like obvious actions, but until I set up these systems, it was easy to deny my need for Relaxation and for nurturing, and many times I worked harder to make my life easier and Created the exact opposite experience.

Daily I take time to Relax. I take one hour a day to do things that allow me to Relax. I call this hour a Love Hour. I use the Love Hour to nurture myself. I take a bath, or go for a walk in nature, or sit reading a book for pleasure, or listen to music for fun, or dance with God/Life/Energy. This Love Hour is such a small commitment to my personal well being. The Love Hour is time I use to develop my connection to God and to expand my experience of God in the world. Sometimes my Love Hour amounts to only 10 minutes, yet my Intention Creates fantastic results.

One simple hour a day energizes me for the rest of my day. That single hour each day gives me ten times the energy to share with others and pursue my dreams. When I take this Love Hour regularly I find that I experience down time less often.

I nurture myself in this process. I release any worry about work, bills, or family and friends. This is time for me to reconnect with my center, with The Feeling of God within me. I take this time to focus on my connection to everything around me. I imagine my connection to the vast expanse of The Feeling of God. I experience feelings of Joy when I feel Whole and Complete and feel Certain in the moment.

When I live in the present moment there is nothing to worry about. The past does not affect me when I live in the present moment. The past can only come into the present when I call my memories to me. The future does not affect me when I live in the moment either. The future can only come into the present when I Choose to allow it to do just that. Living in the moment is the experience of being without connection to my past or future; living the feelings actually in each and every new moment of Now.

I sing more, dance more, laugh more, love more, and I do as many of these each day as possible. When life seems to be too serious, it is my thoughts about a situation that make it serious. The more serious I take life, the less I find I AM truly living, loving, and experiencing life. When life gets too serious, I take my favorite song and sing it with all my heart. This allows me to Relax and reconnect with The Feeling of God in ways that empower me.

The voice of God Gives Ongoing Direction within me each and every moment. This voice reminds me of what is possible in my experience. Many times the suggestion is only a whisper. The suggestion through the voice of God Giving Ongoing Direction is generally Relaxed when presenting a possibility. There is rarely any urgency to the suggestions of the voice of God.

I hear the voice most effectively when I AM Relaxed. When my urgent, bustling thoughts are calm and Relaxed, my intuition offers simple suggestions pointing me in the direction of what is possible when I Choose to follow the prompting. Many times this is the way towards my Oneness with all in my experience.

The exception to this rule applies when the voice makes a Command of Awareness. A Command of Awareness is very pronounced, sometimes uncomfortable or urgent, and rarely can it be cast off as easily as the Relaxed Yes suggestions. A Command of Awareness calls for immediate action to keep others or myself safe from physical harm: "Stop" "Move" "Turn" "Jump" "Run".

My Oneness increases as I follow the voice of God Giving Ongoing Direction within me on a regular basis. I Choose to Create a Relaxed place and act with the knowledge that my intuition is guiding me. My intuition delights in guiding me, knows my desires in life, and is preparing the way for my Oneness with all. My Oneness always in all ways expresses fully who and what I AM - I AM God in expression - I AM Greatness Oneness Demonstrated.

The Feeling of God produces my results effortlessly when I Relax and live in the moment. The Feeling of God produces the Perfect outcome without any extra work from me to Create my imagined good. As I follow the suggestions of the voice of God Giving Ongoing Direction within me, I find that The Feeling of God has gone before me to attract the Perfect people, places, and things. Many times the forms that come into my experience are different from the ones I imagined, however they Create the feelings I desire nonetheless. My Feelings of Joy connect me with my Joy and Potential.

To encourage the presence of The Feeling of God in my life, I ask God to Create the Perfect results for me around any issue of concern. Many nights, just before I go to sleep, I Relax by reading spiritually uplifting material and then as I AM about to retire, I give thanks and know with certainty that The Feeling of God is producing the Perfect results in my life for any issue of concern. Most times, the Perfect results are different from my imagined conclusions.

When I have a decision to make in a short span of time, I check to Observe whether or not I AM Relaxed. If I AM Relaxed, I ask my question, listen to, and then follow the suggestions that come to me. However if I am not Relaxed, I take this as a sign to make my decision when I AM Relaxed.

Everything happens in the Perfect way and at the Perfect time. Most of the things that are Perfect and encourage my Oneness have a total calm and Relaxed feeling associated with them. When I feel Relaxed I continue to Create Relaxed experiences.

I AM RELAXED

Instead of Rejecting the things
I do not want to experience,
I Accept everything as
a part of my experience, then
I Select the ways I feel
in my personal experience, because
I understand every experience
is Perfect through God

Surrender comes by Choosing to consciously release
my self~created limitations associated
with my imagined needs.

I AM SURRENDER

I AM Relaxed. I let go of my emotional attachments to particular people, places, and things and let The Feeling of God attract the Perfect people, places, and things.

I Surrender to the wisdom of God. When I Surrender to the wisdom of The Feeling of God, I Create even greater experiences than I had imagined.

In my past, I used to reject the things I did not want to experience. Now I Surrender to them and accept that every thing is a part of my experience for the Perfect reason. Before I would ask "why" an experience had happened? Now I only ask "How"? How can I utilize God/Life/Energy to Create Oneness in my experience Right Here Right Now? From my decision, I select the feelings I AM going to Create in my experiences because I know that Perfect is the way God makes every experience.

My Choice of Surrender is a conscious Choice. Many times, my ego works over time trying to encourage me to change my decision. My ego tells me I lose out on many opportunities by deciding to Surrender to God. In my past, I let my ego convince me of this truth because I did not Choose to Observe my Oneness with God and the powerful truth in that relationship.

Surrender is not Choosing to deny my needs. For in reality, I have no needs. I may have preferences, but I have no needs. God supplies everything needed for the continuation of my life. Life is eternal. My experience of God and Life transforms through my changing perception.

Through Surrender, I Choose to release my self-created limitations associated with my imagined needs. For years I thought my needs were not being met. However, my needs are always being met. What had not been met were my imagined needs. My imagined needs included all the people, place, and things that I desired in my experience. However, the particular forms I imagined limited the ways God could bring my experiences to me.

This had been particularly true in my relationships. For years I imagined the forms I desired in my relationships. It was a particular person, or it was a particular type of person whom would bring me my joy. I worked to make my imagined needs a reality. Through relationships I tried to get everything to match my imagined needs. When my imagined needs were not met, I would withhold things from other people, I would fight with other people, or I would leave people and move into different relationships.

Surrender is my Choice to release the things that continue the illusion of separation from others and from God. Surrender is releasing my emotional attachments to particular people, places, and things. Any expectations I hold onto encourage my separation. Whereas my Freedom from expectation encourages my Oneness.

God attracts the Perfect people, places, and things for my experience. My life changes immediately when I let go of my imagined needs. Once I let go of particular people, places, and things, I realize that God attracts the Perfect people, places, and things for my experience. Many times the forms the Perfect people, places, and things take are far from my imagined needs. However these forms unmistakably Create the feelings I desire.

I AM Surrender when I Choose to focus my energy on the feelings I experience instead of the forms. Surrender occurs when I release my imagined needs and Enjoy my feelings experienced in every moment of Now. I AM Relaxed.

I AM SURRENDER

How can I utilise God/Life/Energy to Create Oneness in my experience Right Here Right Now?

All of my Feelings
are Expressions of Love.

Some Feelings Express
my perceived lack of Love.

Other Feelings Express
my perceived Abundance of Love.

I AM OBSERVATION

I AM Relaxed. I AM Surrender. I AM The Feeling of God in all my thoughts, feelings, words, and actions. The Feeling of God constantly provides everything in my life. The Feeling of God is the *tingle* I feel when I begin a new relationship, the *elation* I feel when things are going well, the Timelessness and Joy I experience when I AM being who and what I AM, which is The Feeling of God.

My contemplation of my world Creates my world. Whatever I contemplate is what I Create, whether I contemplate my perceived good or bad experiences. For this very reason, imagination is a very powerful tool for Creating my experience. In fact, imagination is Creation.

Imagination is the process I use to co-create with God/Life/Energy. I Create everything I focus upon. When I imagine a particular outcome and work towards that outcome, without limiting the forms or process to that particular outcome, many things come to me in even better forms and processes than I originally envisioned.

In every moment of Now, I can Observe whatever my imagination can envision in my experience. What I give to life is what I live in life. In every moment of Now, life provides opportunities for my individual Observation of The Feeling of God. My Observation is different from everyone else's Observation. There is no right or wrong Observation. There is only Observation. However I do recognize forms of Observation, which empower me to fully express The Feeling of God within me.

I AM God, and in every moment of Now The Feeling of God works through me. My experiences meet me at the level I AM prepared for. I can observe anger, pain, Love, Joy, or any other form that I perceive through me. All of these expressions are brought to Awareness through my Observation of The Feeling of God within me. Anything I Observe, I give God/Life/Energy to its formation.

For years, I told myself that certain forms of experience were negative and I repressed particular forms of expression until they grew too large for me to hold back. For years, I could not understand how the expression of my anger could be positive. Only when my expression of anger in my life had become unproductive did I decide to take the time to Observe and discover the productive nature behind it. Discovering the productive side to my anger encouraged me to Observe and discover the productive sides to other forms of expression, which I had felt were negative as well. I had not been able to Observe how these expressions were a necessary part of Creating the Oneness of who and what I AM.

Life is cyclical. This circle of life is made up of numerous experiences, much like pieces in a pie. Those pieces of pie are made up of seemingly opposite characteristics: doubt and belief, reject and accept, give and receive, love and hate, fear and faith. When I view life from a perspective of separation, those characteristics are separate pieces of Life's pie. However, when I view life from a perspective of Unity all of God/Life/Energy's characteristics come together to make up the Oneness Circle of my Life.

From a very young age, I was taught rules concerning right and wrong. As I have grown in age and experience, I have Observed that the lines between right and wrong can shift and disappear. The idea that one thing is good or bad is always Observed from my personal perspective and influenced by my beliefs. Something is good or bad by my Choice alone.

When the Choice I make is to Observe a thing as wrong or different from me, I Create separation. The extreme side of Choosing to Observe something as wrong, different, or separate is conditional judgement.

When the Choice I make is to Observe a thing as similar or another part of the whole, I Create Unity. The extreme side of Choosing to Observe something as right, similar, or unified is Unconditional Love.

God is Unconditional Love in every situation. God does not see one thing as right and another as wrong. From the perspective of God, everything just is. Everything is a part of God's Oneness. There is no separation. There is no right or wrong. There is only God - Greatness Oneness Demonstrated. Although anything can be Observed in my experience by my Choices alone, I Choose to Observe God and Unconditional Love in every situation.

For years, I worked at the level of a human being trying to become one with God. From my perspective I Observed and believed in separation. However, I AM a part of the Oneness that is God. There can only be separation, when I Choose to believe in it and Create it through my own thoughts, feelings, words, and actions.

I AM God/Life/Energy. As God/Life/Energy, I realize that there is no right or wrong. This becomes more evident when I talk about my Observation of feelings. No matter what feeling I express, I AM God. Whether I express anger, sorrow, pain, joy, or happiness I AM just an expression of God/Life/Energy.

My Observation of God/Life/Energy in the forms of feelings can be anything other than just expression. As a youth, I believed certain expressions were inappropriate. As an adult, I understand that certain expressions are less productive to Create what I desire to Create when they are compared to other expressions.

Feelings that manifest through me are my natural reactions to my experience. What I do with my feelings can be less than natural.

Repression is one of the least productive Choices I have used in my experience. Whenever I repress a feeling that wishes to come out, it works for a time, but eventually that feeling comes out in one form or another. By example, when I have repressed anger in my past, it eventually expressed itself in some form. One of the resulting forms has been a larger expression of anger directed at others. Another had been an unconscious transference of anger onto myself. I may be mad at another, but I unconsciously take the anger out on myself for not being able to express my feelings to that other. Another has been physical illness. These are some of the reasons whereby repression Creates challenges in my life.

The Feeling of God is constantly working through me. In fact, I Observe that The Feeling of God manifests in my expressions of pain, sorrow, anger, or Joy to Create Balance for me Always in All Ways. As a result, when I feel happy, I express it.

When I feel unhappy, I express it. The process of life is expressing my present feelings in every moment of Now. The more I AM in touch with my present feelings, the more I AM in touch with The Feeling of God within me.

In every moment of Now, I Never Overlook Whatsoever the opportunity provided by The Feeling of God within me to be who and what I AM. When I feel something I express it. When I express it, it helps Create Balance within me. Whenever I express a feeling, it is finished. There is little need to express the memories of a feeling again because each and every moment is full of new feelings to be experienced. I can express my feelings unconsciously or Consciously.

Unconscious expression of my feelings maybe directed at others or myself. Unconscious expressions foster a victim mentality. Unconscious expressions support pain and separation from God/Life/Energy.

Conscious expressions of my feelings maybe used for Balance and Centering. Conscious expressions foster a Victor mentality. Conscious expressions support Joy and Unity with God/Life/Energy.

This is very simple with small challenges in my life. I express my feelings to easily return to a Centered state. I use this same process with large challenges in my life, however my perception of my feelings can be different. I perceive betrayal by a coworker to be at a different feeling level when compared to betrayed by a loved one.

From the perspective of God, all experiences encourage me to express my feelings to Create Balance and Unity within God/Life/Energy.

Focusing on my feelings is different from expression. When I focus on a feeling, many times I become trapped by that experience. I replay it over and over and the feeling grows to one extreme or another because it is continually being fostered. If the feeling is anger, it continues to grow and can become difficult to Center when it reaches violence. If the feeling is Joy, it continues to grow and becomes difficult to Center when it reaches fantasy.

When I utilize my imagination to replay situations I wish

could have been different, this form of focus on my feelings traps me in a memory loop. Whenever I find myself caught up in a memory loop, I direct my focus onto things I can Create in this moment right Now.

In life, I experience a whole range of feelings. My feelings come in different ways and at different times. Feelings are a very natural part of life, but what I Choose to do with them can be unnatural. It is unnatural to repress my feelings. It is unnatural to focus on my feelings. In my past, I have tried to repress the feelings I wished were different and I have focused on the feelings I wished to encourage.

I have Observed that this process seems to work until the day the repressed feelings come to the forefront of my experience. My anger, pain, sorrow, Joy, or Elation can come through me at what seems a very inappropriate time. An example of this occurs when a friend has a serious problem and I find I AM moved to giggle. My giggle is my reaction to the serious nature of a friend's experience. In this experience, The Feeling of God is trying to Center my energy. Sometimes this expression allows the other person to see the situation with humor and less seriousness also.

My giggle expression is often easier to understand than my anger expression. An example of my anger occurs when I am asked by a friend to help him move. On the day I am helping, the original morning work of five hours turns into an extra two hours after lunch as well. My anger grows when I cannot keep my plans for the afternoon. I may feel obliged to continue helping with the move, while I am angry with myself that I needed to allow for extra time in this situation. Also I may be angry (with myself again) that my afternoon appointment is going to be missed. However, instead of expressing my truth with the friend I am helping, I may Choose to work harder to complete the move as quickly as possible. But if my frustration slips out, the moving event can become the focal point for my anger.

I AM Creating My Own Answers when I develop systems that minimize my extremes of energy expression. To reduce my self-created stress, I accept that for my Relaxed experience of life one major event a day helps me Create Oneness with everything in my experience.

Through my increased Awareness in my experience, I constantly Observe expressions of my personal light and shadow. These apparent opposites are in reality the extremes of my personal inner expression taking physical form. The Feeling of God within me Creates my Observed outer experiences. Wherever I place my energy using my thoughts, feelings, words, and actions is also the place my Creative energy manifests. The shadows in my experience are there for me to accept as a part of my entire being. My wholeness comes when I Choose to Unify the opposites I have Observed in my experience.

The extreme shadows that I encounter in my experience are reminders for me to accept those shadows within myself as a part of the Oneness Circle of my Life. At times, I may see things outside of me and say I am not like that. I am not greedy, jealous, or violent. However, I AM Observation and I can only Observe outside of me things that are a part of me as well. Without identifying at some level with greed, jealousy, and violence, they would be perceived as Only Love.

In my past, I thought that some of my feelings were to be repressed or denied. Now, whenever I become afraid to feel my shadow feelings, they begin to rule me. Every shadow that I repress gains strength until the shadow becomes larger than the light within me and then all I experience is shadows. When I Observe shadows in my experience, I Love them and allow them to be a part of my Oneness without needing to Choose them. When I Observe the Light in my experience, I Align with, Allow, and Accept more Light as my Core. I AM Relaxed. I AM Surrender.

I AM OBSERVATION

Conscious expressions of my feelings are used for Balance and Centering. Conscious expressions foster a Victor mentality. Conscious expressions support Joy and Unity with God/ Life/ Energy.

My Balance is Created by Selecting the feelings that come up for me as the feelings I Choose to experience.

I AM BALANCE

I AM Relaxed. I AM Surrender. I AM Observation. My outer world is Created from my inner world. My inner beliefs are most easily associated with my feelings. My inner feelings attract the forms that make up my outer experience. When I Observe that my inner feelings are of worry and unhappiness, the outer forms I attract allow me to experience more worry and unhappiness. Similarly when I Observe my inner feelings are of Joy and Contentment, the outer forms I attract allow me to experience more Joy and Contentment.

No matter what forms I experience, I Consciously Choose the feelings I wish to Create. In each moment I experience different feelings. The quicker I Choose the feelings that come up as the feelings I wish to Create, the sooner I understand my Path of Oneness with The Feeling of God.

In the process of Creating my own answers, I have been caught up in the Balance of right and wrong. However, Balance is not about the validity of different Choices. Every Choice is right in and of itself. Balance is found in the common ground of different Choices. The similarities and the Unity of differences show the Oneness in particular situations.

To clearly see the similarities in different situations, I Choose to be honest about my feelings in those various situations. This means I Choose to understand the feelings of different Choices rather than the forms of those Choices. When I have a decision to make between helping a friend or not helping a friend. The form of the Choice seems very simple: help or not help. I believe the feelings behind my dilemma are just as simple to understand: feel good about Choosing to help or feel good about Choosing not to help. As the experience plays out, however, I find that my Choice to help or not, and my Choice to feel good about it are not the same.

There are different feelings involved in all Choices. And in both of these Choices I am concerned with the way the other person might react to my Choices. Whether I help or not has a lot to do with the way I feel I might be perceived. My Choice has very little to do with my feelings. My Choices are concerned with my perception of the other person's feelings. Because of my past Observations, whenever a decision involving another person comes up, I consciously look to become aware that my Choices are based on what feels right for me.

When another person is not involved in my Choice, the Balance between feelings and forms is just as important. By example, when I AM prepared to purchase something new, I may see this Choice as making me feel good or I may feel guilty for my desire.

There is no right or wrong. There is only experience. Buying a new toy because my old one is broken is different from buying a new toy because my old one is boring. Giving away my boring toy to someone who finds it exciting and then buying a new toy to Create a new experience is a form of Balance. They are only different approaches to Balance.

These forms of Balance are very effective when certain things come into my life. I may receive gifts in my life. These gifts replace an older model or a toy that I no longer use. When I pass along the older things to people who can use them, I encourage the Universal flow of God/Life/Energy in my life.

The Balance and flow of Energy in the Universe often occurs in response to things that I give away. Whatever I Give, I Live. When I share my energy and give to others, similar feeling experiences come back to me from other sources. When I Give with Joy and Celebration, I Live with Joy and Celebration.

However, if I use this process with any expectation of what I receive in return, the experience comes to me at the same level I originally give. In actuality this is not giving - this is expecting. When I Give with expectation, I Live with expectation.

The greatest experience of Balance in my life is demonstrated when I respond to challenges. When I go to one extreme or the other it is very difficult for me to hear the voice of God Giving Ongoing Direction, much less follow it. As a result, Balance occurs when I AM Relaxed and I Surrender to The Feeling of God Giving Ongoing Direction within me. I AM a powerful example for others when I effectively Balance the extreme feelings that come up in my life. I AM Greatness Oneness Demonstrated when I Balance my entire experience. I AM Relaxed. I AM Surrender. I AM Observation.

I AM BALANCED

I Create Harmony in my life by expressing one third of my energy in three areas of my life: physical, mental, and spiritual.

I AM HARMONY

I AM Relaxed. I AM Surrender. I AM Observation. I AM Balance. I Create Harmony when I Unify the three areas that form my life: mind, body, and spirit. I Consciously Create Harmony through my Choices.

I Create Harmony in my body through my daily Choices. I Choose to make Healthy Choices for my body through my eating, my exercise, and my Habits. I Choose to eat Healthy foods that provide energy in the most effective forms. I Choose to be active on a regular basis. I Choose to maintain Healthy Habits.

I Create Harmony in my mind through my daily Choices. I Choose to read books that encourage my Joy and Potential on a regular basis in areas of interest concerning my dreams and goals in life. I Choose to take courses that are geared toward my purpose. Every activity I Choose inspires me to Be and Create who and what I AM - I AM God (Greatness Oneness Demonstrated).

I Create Harmony in my spirit through my daily Choices. I Choose to Consciously Connect with God/Life/Energy. I Choose to meditate daily. I Choose to pray with Gratitude for all the things in my life. I Choose to Bless everything in my life. I Choose to Align with, Allow, and Accept my Unity with all things in my life.

I Create Harmony in my life by expressing one third of my energy in each of these areas of my life. In my past, I focused on one of the areas more than the others and I became physically, mentally, or spiritually adept, while the other areas of my life fell by the wayside. Now I Choose to Harmonize these areas in my life. I listen to the voice of God Giving Ongoing Direction in my life reminding me which areas can benefit from additional attention.

First thing in the morning, I Choose to acknowledge the Perfect Harmony of my day. I acknowledge my Connection to God. I Choose to Bless my day and all its Abundance before it arrives.

At the end of my day, I Choose activities that encourage Love and Harmony in my life. I Choose to express Love with my family and friends or I Choose to be intimate with significant others. Some days, I Choose to read spiritually uplifting books before I go to bed, because all the energy in my final experiences of each day play in my head throughout the night. I Choose my experiences to Manifest in an easy and relaxed manner for All That Is. I AM Relaxed. I AM Surrender. I AM Observation. I AM Balance.

I AM HARMONY

I Create Harmony in my body
through my daily Choices.

I Create Harmony in my mind
through my daily Choices.

I Create Harmony in my spirit
through my daily Choices.

When I Choose to Observe
Only Love in an experience
that is what I Create.

I AM FORGIVENESS

I AM Relaxed. I AM Surrender. I AM Observation. I AM Balance. I AM Harmony. There is only one person to ever forgive in my life - myself. I forgive myself for my mistakes, grudges, hurts, and disappointments, which are only my interpretations of my past. I forgive myself for my fears, worries, and doubts, which are only my interpretations of my future. I live a life of adventure in the Present moment.

In my past, I believed that it was other people I had to forgive. However the pain, anger, or other feelings I associated with my past experiences, were only my inner experience of them. The situations that did not work out the way I imagined they should have were painful inside of me only until I Chose to let go of my painful perceptions of them.

Every experience is the Perfect experience of Unconditional Love in expression. I Choose to perceive experiences as expressing either a lack of Love or an Abundance of Love in my life. It is always my Choice. I may say that society thinks a certain way, or my family believes a certain reaction is called for, but it is my decision to Choose what I think and believe concerning every experience in my life. I Choose the meaning for all of my experiences.

Whatever I Choose to Observe in an experience is what I Create for that experience. I AM Forgiveness when I Choose to view my past experiences from my present perspective, which perceives an Abundance of Love. When I Choose to Observe Only Love in an experience that is what I Create. No matter what occurs in my life, every experience happens in the right way and at the right time for my development.

I can Choose to forgive anything Right Now. Creating immediate forgiveness allows me to Create Balance in my experience. I Choose to express my feelings in the present moment (whatever they may be) and Choose to no longer focus on my past feelings. Whenever I have focused on past situations by living in a memory loop of bad or good experiences that is what I continued to Create - living in a memory loop. Instead of living and expressing my version of Love, Life, and God Right Now, I AM watching someone (me in my past memory) express a past version of Love, Life, and God.

Some experiences seem too bad to Forgive and my ability to Forgive a particular situation may take a long time to develop, but whenever it does, it is the Perfect time. I can recognise the ways The Feeling of God makes me Whole and Complete Now. Recollection of repressed memories is one way to love and heal them. Recollection is not the only way to love and heal myself. All memories I do recall are provided for me only when and if I am ready and able to work through them. All challenging memories that I recall are given when I AM able to heal them.

Forgiveness takes different forms. Sometimes Forgiveness takes place with the particular people, yet Forgiveness only needs to take place within me. When I Choose to Forgive my interpretation of a past experience, and the Forgiveness has taken place within me, my outer experience mirrors my inner interpretation. When I fully Forgive myself for a bad relationship in my past, and meet up with that person again the separation is healed. The only work I did was to fully Imagine Forgiveness and Unity within myself and that becomes Manifest in my outer experience.

To heal the separation I feel from others actually means healing the separation I feel from God. I ask the voice of God Giving Ongoing Direction within me to show me what I need to know to move effectively forward. This answer may come immediately, but sometimes this answer comes in the next day or week or month. Yet it always comes in the Perfect way and at the Perfect time.

Sometimes weeks after a question is posed, the voice of God Giving Ongoing Direction suggests a new experience I Can Be, Do, or Have. When I follow that guidance, I meet a friend I have not seen in years, or I encounter a book I had never seen before, or I decide to take a course in a new area of interest. Although these things usually have no relation to my original question, the friend says something I need to hear, the book opens to a page with the necessary information, or the course mirrors my experience in a similar form. My response always comes in the Perfect people, places, and things for my healing and unity within God.

Always in all ways my forgiveness Creates Unity from my separation. My Forgiveness heals my separation from people in my past, and when we come together again we are connected. The separation is only my Observation of my experience, it is not my actual experience.

Forgiveness always suggests what is possible. I Can Choose to Forgive my interpretation of a past situation. Forgiveness does not say I Must Choose to Forgive another. Forgiveness reminds me that it is possible to Choose happiness and peace of mind in this moment concerning any and every situation. I AM Creating My Own Answers. I AM Creating a life of Adventure. I AM Relaxed. I AM Surrender. I AM Observation. I AM Balance. I AM Harmony.

I AM FORGIVENESS

Forgiveness reminds me that it is possible to Choose happiness and peace of mind in this moment concerning any and every experience.

I AM GRATEFUL

I AM Relaxed. I AM Surrender. I AM Observation. I AM Balance. I AM Harmony. I AM Forgiveness. Every experience in every moment of Now is Perfect. It is only my perception of an experience as being good or bad that makes it appear so. Love, Life and God are only words used to describe everything in the Universe. I AM One within All That Is. When I perceive something as being separate from me, my perception becomes my Intention for my Life. Love, Life and God are never ending and never apart. There is Only Love, Only Life, Only God, and Only Oneness.

I AM Grateful for my perception of Oneness. Through my perception of Oneness and my Gratefulness for that Unity, I Create my experiences. I AM Love. I AM Life. I AM God. I AM That I AM.

Whenever I experience something that I perceive as different from me, as separate from me, I AM Grateful for the gentle reminder of God Giving Ongoing Direction within me which says, I AM THAT I AM. When I perceive that another person is behaving in a way that I perceive as different (separate from me) I remind myself - I AM THAT person I AM. When I perceive anything in my experience as occurring in any way that I perceive as different (separate from me) I remind myself - I AM THAT perception I AM. I AM One with Everything.

I AM Grateful for every experience in my life. When I wake up in the morning, I Embody a Feeling of Gratitude and Thank God for the day before me, which is Perfect in its design. I AM Relaxed with my knowledge that everything is Perfect. From my Grateful and Relaxed beginning to each day, I easily Surrender to my Expression of God in a Balanced way. Every different or challenging experience that comes to me is easier to accept from a loving and Grateful state of being.

I AM the One who perceives my experiences. I AM the One who decides whether my experiences are good or bad. I AM the One who gives my experiences meaning. When I AM Grateful for my experiences and give them a meaning of Perfection that is what I Create. I Create the Perfection in the forms of my experience by perceiving experiences as my Blessings in disguise.

At the end of my day, I consciously recount the things I AM Grateful for in my day. I AM Relaxed. I AM Surrender. I AM Observation. I AM Balance. I AM Harmony. I AM Forgiveness.

I AM GRATEFUL

I AM Grateful for the gentle reminder of God Giving Ongoing Direction within me which says: "I AM That I AM."

I Accept my previous limitations
as a point to expand from
and enable myself to
powerfully Create
in ways that are
Limitless.

I AM ACCEPTANCE

I AM Relaxed. I AM Surrender. I AM Observation. I AM Balance. I AM Harmony. I AM Forgiveness. I AM Grateful. Acceptance is a powerful tool for Creating Oneness. Every experience that shows up in my life reminds me that I can Accept it Unconditionally as a part of the Oneness of All That Is.

In the Oneness Circle of life, experiences provide opportunities to always further express who and what I AM - I AM God. All experiences provide me with the opportunity to Accept my own limitations and expand from them and Create in ways that are limitless. Whether I believe an experience is about others or myself, the Choice is always mine to Choose what I can Create from any point in my experience.

When I perceive other people as being different, it is only a judgement. I Accept that everyone is expressing God through their experience. I may not understand how another person's expression is God, and others may not understand my expression of God. I do not expect or need them too. Instead I allow others to be who and what they are (whatever that may be), which is a Perfect individuation of God.

The Acceptance I AM Creating in my life occurs when I allow other people to be their expression of God always in all ways. When I try to change others, I am forgetting my truth. My truth Creates my life. My truth is mirrored in my experience with others. My truth is built inside me. My truth is not Created by changing the people, places, and things around me.

By example, in my past, when I left a particular relationship and went into a new one, I imagined that the new relationship would be different. However the relationship may have been with a different partner, but I was still the same person. My relationships mirror my inner beliefs in relationships. Unless I change my beliefs, my new relationship becomes similar to the old one because it still mirrors my inner beliefs about relationships.

Sometimes it is easier for me to believe my inner truth when I Choose new outer experiences, which allow me to Accept my inner truth more effectively. However, I AM Aware that that is me Choosing new beliefs through action.

My experiences are good or bad through my perception of them. All my experiences are made up of the same Unconditional Loving energy of the Universe. I can perceive that Energy as being either good or bad because of my ideas of what I Observe I AM experiencing in my life.

Life provides me with the Perfect opportunities to Create the experiences I believe are going to bring me Joy. When I Accept that every experience provides me with the Perfect opportunity to experience Peace, Love, and Joy, that is what I Create.

In my past, I perceived my experiences as taking me away from the particular people, places, and things that I imagined were going to bring me Joy. However the Energy of the Universe always attracts the Perfect people, places, and things for me to fulfil my purpose. The forms are often very different than the ones I envision Create my Joy. The Energy of the Universe is Unconditional. As a result, the Universe Creates experiences which allow me to Accept my experience that Life is set up for everyone to win.

Accepting every experience as an opportunity to Create my experiences, Creates that very experience. I Accept everything as the Perfect opportunity to Create my experience. I Accept my perceptions as the point from which I can expand to Create limitless experiences. Do my perceptions encourage me to hold onto Feelings that continue to Create experiences dealing with similar Feelings? Or do my perceptions empower me to Accept everyone as the Perfect people, places, and things to Create my dreams?

The Feelings of my experience are more powerful than the forms. When I get frustrated because particular forms are not coming into my life, that frustration attracts future frustrating forms to my experience. When I Understand and Accept that my Calm feelings Attract similar feeling experiences that is what I Create.

Everything in my life encourages me to Accept them Unconditionally. I Accept my previous limitations as a point to expand from. All experiences enable me to powerfully Create in ways that are limitless. I AM Relaxed. I AM Surrender. I AM Observation. I AM Balance. I AM Harmony. I AM Forgiveness. I

AM Grateful.

I AM ACCEPTANCE

What I Give to life is what I Live in life.
I Give Blessings and I Live Blessings.

I AM BLESSING

I AM Relaxed. I AM Surrender. I AM Observation. I AM Balance. I AM Harmony. I AM Forgiveness. I AM Grateful. I AM Acceptance. No matter what my experiences are, no matter the ways I Observe them, I Bless them all. For what I give to life I live in life. I Give Blessings and I Live Blessings.

I Bless all people. I Bless all places. I Bless all things. I Bless all my experiences. Everything in my experience is a Blessing when I perceive it that way. Every day in every way my experiences grow in their Blessings.

My most challenging experiences are also my most powerful Blessings. In my past, relationships have ended, trips have changed, and possessions have been lost, but in hindsight the people, places, and things that replaced them allowed me to more fully express who and what I AM.

Wherever I place my energy that is what I Create. I Bless every situation and that is what I Create. In my past, I have Observed perceived challenges until I remembered that the experience was actually the Perfect opportunity and Blessed the experience. My Blessing allows me to experience the situation without accepting it as good or bad. Every opportunity is better than good, better than great, it is the Perfect opportunity. I Bless every opportunity.

Every experience is a Blessing in disguise until I Choose to Observe the Blessing in every moment of Now. This becomes easier and easier when I Bless my experience immediately. I Bless it Now.

I Bless the people, places, and things in my experience and the Perfect people, places, and things Bless me. I Bless others without any expectation in return. I Bless others because I can. I Bless people, places, and things in my experience because I perceive that I AM Complete in every moment of Now. I recognise that I AM God and that everyone in my experience is God. Every single thing is an aspect of God and I continue to Bless every aspect of God.

My Blessing comes through The Feeling of God within me.

I AM Relaxed. I AM Surrender. I AM Observation. I AM Balance. I AM Harmony. I AM Forgiveness. I AM Grateful. I AM Acceptance.

I AM BLESSING

Every experience is a Blessing in disguise until
I Choose to Observe the Blessing
in every moment of Now.

All people, places, and things are
Only Love,
Only Life,
Only God,
Only Oneness.

I AM THE PERFECT PEOPLE, PLACES, AND THINGS

I AM Relaxed. I AM Surrender. I AM Observation. I AM Balance. I AM Harmony. I AM Forgiveness. I AM Grateful. I AM Acceptance. I AM Blessing. The Forms of God come to me through the Perfect people, places, and things.

All people in my experience are my mirrors. They are tangible examples of who I AM on a daily basis. My inner beliefs are mirrored in the outer world by the people who come to me. If I believe that a person is anything but Only Love, that is because inside me I am still anything but Only Love. This is not good or bad, this is just my experience.

To become God within my experience, I perceive everyone as Only Love. It is my perception of a person that makes them anything but Only Love. Every person is Only Love. I can Choose to remove my limitations that perceive anything but Only Love in expression.

In my past, I perceived it was easier to see other people as evil in comparison to myself. I perceived these people as different, but they always mirrored my thoughts in experience. My refusal to see my own inner greed, jealousy, and judgment became mirrored in other people. I perceived these feelings as bad and tried to repress them. This focus continued to Create similar experiences for me to Only Love.

Now I recognise that the Perfect people come into my life to remind me of my inner perceptions, which Create my experience. I can accept a perception of evil and continue to Create experiences that mirror my inner perception, or I can select a perception of Only Love and continue to Create experiences that mirror that inner perception. The Choice is mine. I Choose to view different behaviours through my inner perceptions. The beauty of others increases when my inner belief of their beauty increases. What I believe is what I perceive and what I achieve in my experience with others when I believe in Only Love, I perceive Only Love, and I achieve Only Love.

All places in my experience are the Perfect places. I find that some places are naturally Perfect. Some places exude Only

Love. For me, beaches exude Only Love. Forests exude Only Love. Mountains exude Only Love. These places are easily understood as the Perfect places. Yet no matter what place I AM in, it is always the Perfect place for me to express who and what I AM. In all places I AM Only Love. I AM God.

In my past, I believed and perceived many things other than Only Love, and I achieved many things other than Only Love. Now I believe and perceive Only Love in everything and that is what I achieve.

By example, I have been in places that seemed dangerous and the people around me seemed less than loving, but I held firm to my belief of Only Love, of God. I Choose to perceive Only Love in the people, places, and things and I achieve Only Love.

If I perceive a place as less than loving that is my Chosen perception about a place. Belief and perception are interchangeable. Whether I believe something first and perceive it second or perceive it first and believe it second, the same result manifests. Therefore, I Choose to believe and perceive Only Love even before my experiences arrive, and Only Love is what I achieve.

All things in my experience are the Perfect things. I utilize all things that empower my self-awareness of Only Love. Every tool I utilize in my life is for the purpose of Only Love. I read books that express the principle of Only Love. I utilize First Nations teachings about plants, animals, and the material world that encourage Only Love. I decipher my dreams using principles that encourage Only Love.

When I utilize tools that deal with Only Love, they also remind me of the ways I may perceive anything but love as well. Love is presented in infinite forms. The Universe is Only Love, but my perception of the Universe can be anything other than Only Love when that is what I Choose. I Choose to Observe Only Love and utilize the tools that encourage my perception of Only Love in my experience of God/Life/Energy.

In my past, I perceived Love in two main forms: Abundance of love and lack of love. However, the belief that empowers my life is the belief in Only Love. Every experience is Only Love. In my past, I have Chosen to perceive lack of love and

Abundance of love. Now I Never Overlook Whatsoever the Abundance of Only Love in my experience. There is Only Love Now. There is Only Life Now. There is Only God Now. There is Only Oneness Now. There is Only Greatness Oneness Demonstrated Now.

The Perfect people, places, and things make up the forms of Only Love, Only Life, Only God, Only Oneness. That is all there is. My answers come from everywhere. The entire Universe produces Only Love in every moment of Now. It is my Choice to Choose what I perceive, believe, and achieve. I AM Relaxed. I AM Surrender. I AM Observation. I AM Balance. I AM Harmony. I AM Forgiveness. I AM Grateful. I AM Acceptance. I AM Blessing.

I AM THE PERFECT PEOPLE, PLACES, AND THINGS

There is Only Love Now.

THE ONENESS CARDS

Through the years, I have utilised divination cards of various designs as tools to encourage my Awareness and Oneness with everything in my experience. All the card sets have informed my experience and helped me to Observe my life as an immense Oneness Circle made up of billions of pie pieces.

I have condensed these pie pieces into 100 *I AM* statements. These statements represent powerful, yet separate aspects of my being which I regularly Observe in my life. I previously accepted many of these *I AM* statements as being on the extreme ends of my experience. I AM LOVE. I AM HATE. I AM SAD. I AM HAPPY. I AM ACCEPTANCE. I AM REJECTION. I AM NURTURING. I AM ABUSING.

These statements represent the most common ways I have Chosen to Observe my experience. When I Choose to Reject an Observation, it begins to rule my life. When I Choose to Accept an Observation into the Oneness of who I AM, it makes me whole. My Oneness with everything in experience constantly increases by Choosing Unity with absolutely everything in experience.

On the back three pages of this book are 100 *I AM* statements. If you wish to photocopy these 100 I AM Statements onto a card stock paper, you can download a free pdf at:
www.UnconditionalLoveBooks.com/100IAMStatements.pdf
I cut out these statements and place them into a bowl because the cards easily mix together in a bowl. I pull a Oneness card or cards whenever I feel prompted to. Every card only reminds me about my energy use and Observations in situations, they never tell me about another person's energy use. The orientation of the card or cards I Choose have different reminders.

Regular Card: A card that I pick in the upright or regular orientation reminds me that I AM Uplifting and Encouraging this aspect of Oneness by Consciously directing God/Life/Energy through me.

Reversed Card: A card that I pick up in an upside down or reversed position reminds me that I AM denying this aspect of Oneness by directing my energy onto the people, places, and things around me.

All of the cards have an accompanying affirmation that I use to remind me to Choose Oneness with The Feeling of God in all of my experiences. All of the cards remind me to Observe all my experiences as blessings in disguise. All of the cards remind me to accept Unconditionally all things in my life. All of the cards encourage me to be God, Greatness Oneness Demonstrated.

THE ONENESS CARDS

ONENESS CARD SPREADS AND QUESTIONS

Oneness

How can I utilise The Feeling of God to Create Oneness in my experience right Now?

Balanced Oneness

What masculine/action and feminine/feeling aspects of my being can I balance by perceiving their similarities to Create Oneness in my experience?

1. Masculine/Expression/Word/Action/Outer
2. Feminine/Intuition/Release/Thought/Feeling/Inner

Harmony Oneness

What Physical, Mental, and Spiritual aspects foster Oneness in my life Right Now?

1. Physical
2. Mental
3. Spiritual

Cycle of Oneness

Where am I on the Planting, Nurturing, and Harvesting stages to Oneness with my dream?

1. Planting
2. Nurturing
3. Harvesting

Creation Oneness

How are my Relationships, Abundance, and Health encouraging Oneness?

1. Relationship
2. Abundance
3. Health

Experience Oneness

What Thoughts, Feelings, Words, and Actions encourage my Oneness?

1. Thoughts
2. Feelings
3. Words
4. Actions

Seven Chakra Oneness

How are my seven chakras reminding me to Create Oneness at this time?

7. Crown:	God Giving Ongoing Direction
6. Third eye:	Visualized Unity
5. Throat:	Vocal Expression of Unity
4. Heart:	Unconditional Love Center
3. Solar Plexus:	Feeling of God
2. Navel:	Creation of God
1. Root:	Physical Action

Greatness Oneness Demonstrated

God is reminding me to Select Greatness Oneness Demonstrated.

1. Overview of this experience.
2. My talents in this experience.
3. The reminder in this experience.
4. How to be grateful for this experience.
5. How to Love this experience Unconditionally.
6. My direction to Create Oneness in this experience.
7. How to let God Give Ongoing Direction in this experience.

Choosing Unity over separation in every experience
is the path to world peace and world healing.

Choosing Love over fear in every experience
is the path of Unconditional Love.

When everyone Chooses Unity over
separation and Love over fear,
the resulting manifestation for us all is God,
Global Oneness Demonstrated.

100 I AM STATEMENTS EXPANDED

I AM ABUSING
*When I Observe Abuse, my experience reminds me
to nurture the inner completeness of myself and others.*

I AM ABUNDANCE
*When I Observe Abundance, my experience reminds me that God
Provides all of my Abundance, not any person, place, or thing.*

I AM ACCEPTANCE
*When I Observe Acceptance, my experience reminds me to Accept
that every experience is God's Perfection in limitless ways.*

I AM ACTION
*When I Observe Action, my experience reminds me that
God expresses Love through my Loving Actions.*

I AM ADDICTION
*When I Observe Addiction, my experience reminds me that
God provides the Only Freedom that is permanent.*

I AM ADVENTURE
*When I Observe Adventure, my experience reminds me that I can
Create Adventure by extending just past my comfort zone.*

I AM AGREEING
*When I Observe Agreement, my experience reminds me to listen to
The voice of God Giving Ongoing Direction within me.*

I AM ANGRY
*When I Observe Anger, my experience reminds me that anger is
effectively released through expressing it rather than focusing it.*

I AM ANXIOUS
*When I Observe Anxiousness, my experience reminds me that I
can Choose happiness and Peace of mind in this moment.*

I AM ARGUING
*When I Observe Arguing, my experience reminds me that
I can Choose to be happy instead of right.*

I AM BALANCE
*When I Observe Balance, my experience reminds me to Relax
and Surrender to The Feeling of God to Create Oneness.*

I AM BELIEF
*When I Observe Belief, my experience reminds me that when I
believe and perceive Only Love then Only Love is what I receive.*

I AM BIRTH
*When I Observe Birth, my experience reminds me that I can
Create new birth by expanding from my previous limitations.*

I AM BLESSING
*When I Observe Blessing, my experience reminds me that when
I give Blessings, I live Blessings.*

I CAN
*My experience reminds me I Can be, do, and have
all things through The Feeling of God.*

I AM CAUTIOUS
*When I Observe Caution, my experience reminds me to powerfully
establish my Connection with God Giving Ongoing Direction.*

I AM CLARITY
*When I Observe Clarity, my experience reminds me that Clarity
in any area of my life brings Clarity to every area of my life.*

I AM COMPLEX
*When I Observe Complexity, my experience reminds me to
simplify my perception and expression of my experience.*

I AM CONFIDENT
When I Observe Confidence, my experience reminds me that Confidence inspires me to be the best of who and what I AM.

I AM CONFUSED
When I Observe Confusion, my experience reminds me to simplify my beliefs to encourage my Creations.

I AM CREATIVITY
When I Observe Creativity, my experience reminds me that Creativity fosters my Connection with God.

I AM CURSING
When I Observe Cursing, my experience reminds me to Bless every experience and everyone in it to Create Unity.

I AM CYCLES
When I Observe Cycles, my experience reminds me that I can move through the cycles in my life with Joy and acceptance.

I AM DEATH
When I Observe Death, my experience reminds me in every cycle of life that I can Choose to express Only Love.

I AM DENYING
When I Observe Denial, my experience reminds me to Accept that all experiences are the Perfect experiences to Create Oneness through.

I AM DESTRUCTIVE
When I Observe Destruction, my experience reminds me that I can release all my beliefs that encourage separation from God.

I AM DOUBT
When I Observe Doubt, my experience reminds me that The Feeling of God is my only source and supply.

I AM DREAMS
*When I Observe Dreams, my experience reminds me that
my Dreams Create my reality of Oneness.*

I AM EGO
*When I Observe Ego, my experience reminds me that I can follow
The voice of God Giving Ongoing Direction within me.*

I AM EXPECTING
*When I Observe Expectation, my experience reminds me to release
my imagined needs because all of my needs are met in Oneness.*

I AM FAITH
*When I Observe Faith, my experience reminds me that God
provides everything in the Perfect way and at the Perfect time.*

I AM FEAR
*When I Observe Fear, my experience reminds me that everything
in the Universe is Only Love including this experience.*

I AM FEELINGS
*When I Observe Feelings, my experience reminds me Feelings
are there for me to experience the Oneness and Unity of God.*

I AM FEMININE
*When I Observe Femininity, my experience reminds me to nurture
and love my Connection to The Feeling of God within me.*

I AM FOCUS
*When I Observe intense Focus, my experience reminds me
to focus on perceiving Only Love in my experience.*

I AM FORGIVING
*When I Observe Forgiveness, my experience reminds me that
I can Choose to perceive every experience as Only Love.*

I AM FORMS

When I Observe Forms, my experience reminds me that every form is the Perfect form encouraging my Oneness within God.

I AM FREEDOM

When I Observe Freedom, my experience reminds me to care less about my expectations to live more of my Oneness.

I AM GENEROSITY

When I Observe Generosity, my experience reminds me that my Generosity Aligns with, Allows, and Accepts God's Abundance.

I AM GIVING

When I Observe Giving, my experience reminds me that when I give Blessings, I live Blessings.

I AM GOALS

When I Observe Goals, my experience reminds me that when I define my goals through God, God Creates my goals Perfectly.

I AM GOD

I AM LOVE. I AM LIFE. I AM GOD. I AM ENERGY. I AM Greatness Oneness Demonstrated.

I AM GRATEFUL

When I Observe Gratitude, my experience reminds me that gratitude promotes Unity for all in the human experience.

I AM GREED

When I Observe Greed, my experience reminds me to give generously of God's Abundance provided through me.

I AM HAPPY

When I Observe Happiness, my experience reminds me to Choose Happiness by releasing all experiences to the Perfection of God.

I AM HATE
*When I Observe Hate, my experience reminds me to Love
all things in my experience because I AM that I AM.*

I AM HOLDING
*When I Observe Holding, my experience reminds me to release
my imagined needs to allow God to Create Perfection.*

I AM ILLUSIONS
*When I Observe Illusions, my experience reminds me that
separation is a Chosen Illusion within God's Oneness.*

I AM INNER TRUTH
*When I Observe Inner Truth, my experience reminds me that
I can follow my good feeling Inner Truth at all times.*

I AM INTEGRITY
*When I Observe Integrity, my experience reminds me that all my
thoughts, feelings, words, and actions express my inner truth.*

I AM INTENTION
*When I Observe Intention, my experience reminds me that I can
Intend to manifest Peace, Love, and Joy in all my experiences.*

I AM INSIGNIFICANT
*When I Observe Insignificance, my experience reminds me
that through God my importance is revealed.*

I AM INSINCERE
*When I Observe Insincerity, my experience reminds me that
my Unity within God fosters Honesty and Integrity.*

I AM JOURNEY
*When I Observe Life's Journey, my experience reminds me that my
life Journey changes beliefs of separation into beliefs of Unity*

I AM JUDGING

When I Observe Judgement, my experience reminds me that
I AM forgiving and loving through my experience of Oneness.

I AM KNOWN

When I Observe Knowledge, my experience reminds me that
my past informs my present Choices encouraging Unity.

I AM LISTENING

When I Observe Listening, my experience reminds me that I can
Create a calm space to listen to the voice of God Giving
Ongoing Direction.

I AM LOVE

I AM LOVE. I AM LIFE. I AM GOD. I AM ENERGY.
I AM Greatness Oneness Demonstrated.

I AM MANIFESTATION

When I Observe Manifestation, my experience reminds me that
I Manifest The Feeling of God in all my experiences.

I AM MASCULINE

When I Observe Masculinity, my experience reminds me that I AM
God in Action through my thoughts, feelings, words, and actions.

I AM MIRRORS

When I Observe Mirrors, my experience reminds me that every
thing is a mirror to my inner beliefs - I AM THAT I AM.

I MUST

My experience reminds me that there is nothing I Must
experience. However, I Can Be, Do, and Have all things.

I AM NURTURING

When I Observe Nurturing, my experience reminds me that I can
take the time to Nurture my Connection to God.

I AM OPTIMISTIC

When I Observe Optimism, my experience reminds me that I Observe my glass half full of experiences and half full of unknown experiences.

I AM OUTER TRUTH

When I Observe Outer Truth, my experience reminds me that my Inner Truth Creates my Outer Truth.

I AM PARTICULAR

When I Observe Particularity, my experience reminds me all people, places, and things are Perfect for me.

I AM PATIENCE

When I Observe Patience, my experience reminds me that through patience I experience all forms of Oneness.

I AM PEACEFUL

When I Observe Peace, my experience reminds me that I can Choose Peace of mind and Create Peaceful tranquillity.

I AM PERFECT

When I Observe Perfection, my experience reminds me that all people, places, and things in my life are Perfect.

I AM PESSIMISTIC

When I Observe Pessimism, my experience reminds me that my glass is half-empty to provide room for God's Oneness to manifest.

I AM PHYSICAL

When I Observe Physicality, my experience reminds me to enjoy the ways physical pleasures encourage my experience of Oneness.

I AM PLANS

When I Observe Planning, my experience reminds me to Plan my dreams and then Never Overlook Whatsoever when it shows up.

I AM POVERTY
When I Observe Poverty, my experience reminds me to
Abundantly share of all my gifts because they are limitless.

I AM POWERFUL
When I Observe Power, my experience reminds me that
I AM Powerful through The Feeling of God.

I AM PRAISE
When I Observe Praise, my experience reminds me to
Praise others and myself daily.

I AM PRAYER
When I Observe Prayer, my experience reminds me to
Pray in Gratitude for my Oneness to everything in experience

I AM PURIFICATION
When I Observe Purification, my experience reminds me to
Create Oneness and release my stress through Purifying
experiences.

I AM REACTIONS
When I Observe Reactions, my experience reminds me to
Choose Peace and Love to Create Oneness

I AM RECEIVING
When I Observe Receiving, my experience reminds me that
there is Only Love to receive in every experience.

I AM REJECTION
When I Observe Rejection, my experience reminds me to Accept
my experiences and Select my feelings, because God's Plan is
Perfect.

I AM RELAXED
When I Observe Relaxation, my experience reminds me to
Relax and Surrender to The Feeling of God within me.

I AM RELEASING
When I Observe Release, my experience reminds me that
I can Release my imagined needs to Create wholeness.

I AM SAD
When I Observe Sadness, my experience reminds me that
I can freely express my feelings when they arise.

I AM SEPARATION
When I Observe Separation, my experience reminds me that
all my separate Choices add up to my Oneness.

I AM SILENCE
When I Observe Silence, my experience reminds me that within
Silence, I hear God Giving Ongoing Direction.

I AM SIMPLICITY
When I Observe Simplicity, my experience reminds me to Keep It
Simple Spiritually, Physically, Mentally and Emotionally.

I AM SPIRIT
When I Observe Spirit, my experience reminds me to invoke
the Spirit of God in all my experiences.

I AM SPONTANEITY
When I Observe Spontaneity, my experience reminds me that
when I Choose to do unplanned things, they often go better than
planned.

I AM STAGNANT
When I Observe Stagnation, my experience reminds me that
I can Create my experiences instead of waiting for them.

I AM SURRENDER
When I Observe Surrender, my experience reminds me that
I can let God attract the Perfect people, places, and things.

I AM TALENTS
When I Observe Talents, my experience reminds me to use
my Talents to express and experience God's Joy through me.

I AM TALKING
When I Observe Talking, my experience reminds me
I can use my words to Create and express Only Love.

I AM TENSE
When I Observe Tension, my experience reminds me that
I can Relax because my Essence Attracts my experiences.

I AM THINKING
When I Observe Thinking, my experience reminds me that
I can Think less to Feel more.

I AM UNGRATEFUL
When I Observe Ungratefulness, my experience reminds me that
I can Choose to be Grateful for each and every moment of Now.

I AM UNITY
When I Observe Unity, my experience reminds me that my Unified
thoughts, feelings, words, and actions Create my Oneness.

I AM UNKNOWN
When I Observe the Unknown, my experience reminds me that my
current feelings attract Perfect and Unknown future experiences.

I AM UNYIELDING
When I Observe Unyielding, my experience reminds me that
I can Yield to God's Perfection through and for me.

I AM WISHING
When I Observe Wishing, my experience reminds me that
my wishes are Created when I let go and let God.

I AM WORRIED

When I Observe Worry, my experience reminds me that there is no use worrying because God is my Confidence.

I AM CREATING MY OWN ANSWERS
The ABC's

My **ANSWERS** come through the Perfect People, Places, and Things.

I give **BLESSINGS** and I live **BLESSINGS**.

I **CHOOSE** to experience Only Love, Only Life, Only God, Only Oneness.

The **DREAMS**/doubts I envision become my reality. Where is my focus on my DREAMS/doubts?

I **EXPAND** from my previous limitations to Create in limitless ways.

The **FEELINGS** are more important than the **FORMS**.

GOD Gives Ongoing Direction to Create Greatness Oneness Demonstrated.

I Choose **HAPPINESS** and peace of mind in every moment of Now.

Everything **I** believe and **I** perceive Creates everything **I** achieve.

My **JOYOUS** feelings unite me with God/Life/Energy.

I **KEEP** a Grateful Heart and a Humble Heart.

There is Only **LOVE**, an Abundance of **LOVE**, Unconditional **LOVE**.

When I live in a **MEMORY** loop of experiences that is all I live.

NURTURING my connection to God for one love hour each day empowers me.

ONENESS is Created by accepting everything as a part of my experience.

My **PERCEPTION** of experiences makes them good, bad, or Only Love.

God answers my **QUESTIONS** in the Perfect way at the Perfect time.

I AM **RELAXED** and this Creates more **RELAXED** experiences.

I **SURRENDER** my **SHADOWS** to God to Create my Perfection.

I utilize every **TRUTH** that works in my life until I Create my **TRUTH**.

UNCONDITIONAL LOVE is the Only energy in the universe.

VISUALISING, VOCALISING, and **VITALISING** energizes the framework that Creates my experience.

My **WHOLENESS** comes through Accepting my apparent opposites.

EXPRESSING my feelings is empowering, focussing on them is not.

I **YIELD** to God because everything happens through God's Perfect Plans and Divine Timing.

I share my **ZEST** for living and others share their **ZEST** with me.

I AM CREATING MY OWN ANSWERS
The 123's

The Gifts, Feelings, and Forms of God

1. The Gifts of God: Relax, Surrender, Observation, and Balance.

2. The Feelings of God: Forgiveness, Gratitude, Acceptance, Blessing, and Appreciation.

3. The Forms of God: The Perfect People, Places, and Things.

ABOUT THE AUTHOR

Barry Thomas Bechta is an artist, author, and film maker whose work centers around the concepts of Unconditional Love. Barry knew he wanted to write from a very young age and was encouraged with his artistic skills and only began writing full time in his thirties. He wrote his first book, *I AM Creating My Own Experience* as a personal journal to choose connection with God/Life/Energy. He has since written 17 inspirational spiritual books.

Barry loves to hear from people whom have connected with his writing and used it as a tool to improve their lives. If you would like to write him about your personal experiences as a result of reading any of his books, Barry encourages you to do so.

You can also get a Free Digital Copy of *I AM Creating My Own Experience - The Creation Vibration* from his main website:

www.unconditionallovebooks.com

<u>Unconditional Love Books Titles of Related Interest</u>
<u>by Barry Thomas Bechta</u>

I AM Creating My Own Experience
978-0-9813485-5-1
I AM Creating My Own Answers
978-0-9686835-1-4
I AM Creating My Own Dreams
978-0-9686835-2-1
I AM Creating My Own Relationships
978-0-9686835-3-8
I AM Creating My Own Abundance
978-0-9686835-4-5
I AM Creating My Own Success
978-0-9686835-5-2
I AM Creating My Own Happiness
978-0-9686835-6-9
I AM Creating My Own Experience - The Creation Vibration
978-0-9686835-7-6
I AM Creating My Own Experience - To Manifest Money
978-0-9686835-8-3
I AM Creating My Own Experience - 369 Conscious Days
978-0-9686835-9-0
Loving Oneness
978-0-9813485-0-6
Trust Life
978-0-9813485-1-3
I AM Creating My Own Financial Freedom - The Story
978-0-9813485-2-0
I AM Creating My Own Financial Freedom - The Lessons
978-0-9813485-3-7
Laughing Star's Guide to Laughter, Life, Love, and God
978-0-9813485-4-4

All of the above are books are available through your local
bookstore, or they may be ordered as digital downloads at
www.unconditionallovebooks.com

Barry Thomas Bechta is available for interviews, special events, workshops, and lectures that redefine, guide, and inspire everyone's connection to the Creative Power within themselves. To arrange author interviews, special events, workshops, or lectures, please contact:

UNCONDITIONAL
LOVE BOOKS

Unconditional Love Books
Box # 610 - 2527 Pine St.,
Vancouver, BC, Canada V6J 3E8

info@unconditionallovebooks.com

www.unconditionallovebooks.com

For additional copies of Barry's books, products, and services please contact your local book seller. Many products and services are Only available to order directly from the publisher as eProducts on the website.

Thanks for your purchase and Remember to Consciously Create your Life.

Right Now is the Only Moment of Creation

Enjoy it Fully!

I AM ABUSE	I AM CURSING
I AM ABUNDANCE	I AM CYCLES
I AM ACCEPTANCE	I AM DEATH
I AM ACTION	I AM DENYING
I AM ADDICTION	I AM DESTRUCTIVE
I AM ADVENTURE	I AM DOUBT
I AM AGREEING	I AM DREAMS
I AM ANGRY	I AM EGO
I AM ANXIOUS	I AM EXPECTING
I AM ARGUING	I AM FAITH
I AM BALANCE	I AM FEAR
I AM BELIEF	I AM FEELINGS
I AM BIRTH	I AM FEMININE
I AM BLESSING	I AM FOCUS
I CAN	I AM FORGIVING
I AM CAUTIOUS	I AM FORMS
I AM CLARITY	I AM FREEDOM
I AM COMPLEX	I AM GENEROSITY
I AM CONFIDENT	I AM GIVING
I AM CONFUSED	I AM GOALS
I AM CREATIVITY	I AM GOD

I AM GRATEFUL	I AM OPTIMISTIC
I AM GREED	I AM OUTER TRUTH
I AM HAPPY	I AM PARTICULAR
I AM HATE	I AM PATIENCE
I AM HOLDING	I AM PERFECT
I AM ILLUSIONS	I AM PEACEFUL
I AM INNER TRUTH	I AM PESSIMISTIC
I AM INTEGRITY	I AM PHYSICAL
I AM INTENTION	I AM PLANS
I AM INSIGNIFICANCE	I AM POVERTY
I AM INSINCERE	I AM POWERFUL
I AM JOURNEY	I AM PRAISE
I AM JUDGING	I AM PRAYER
I AM KNOWN	I AM PURIFICATION
I AM LISTENING	I AM REACTIONS
I AM LOVE	I AM RECEIVING
I AM MANIFESTATION	I AM REJECTION
I AM MASCULINE	I AM RELAXED
I AM MIRRORS	I AM RELEASING
I MUST	I AM SAD
I AM NURTURING	I AM SEPARATION

I AM SILENCE

I AM SIMPLICITY

I AM SPIRIT

I AM SPONTANEITY

I AM STAGNANT

I AM SURRENDER

I AM TALENTS

I AM TALKING

I AM TENSE

I AM THINKING

I AM UNGRATEFUL

I AM UNITY

I AM UNKNOWN

I AM UNYIELDING

I AM WISHING

I AM WORRIED

www.ingramcontent.com/pod-product-compliance
Lightning Source LLC
Chambersburg PA
CBHW031522040426
42445CB00009B/359